KU-175-160

The Pocket
Aussie
Fact
Book

The Pocket
Aussie
Fact
Book

MARGARET NICHOLSON

Penguin Books Australia Ltd
487 Maroondah Highway, PO Box 257
Ringwood, Victoria 3134, Australia
Penguin Books Ltd
Harmondsworth, Middlesex, England
Penguin Putnam Inc.
375 Hudson Street, New York, New York 10014, USA
Penguin Books Canada Limited
10 Alcorn Avenue, Toronto, Ontario, Canada M4V 3B2
Penguin Books (N.Z.) Ltd
Cnr Rosedale & Airborne Roads, Albany, Auckland, New Zealand
Penguin Books (South Africa) (Pty) Ltd
5 Watkins Street, Denver Ext 4, 2094, South Africa
Penguin Books India (P) Ltd
11, Commercial Centre, Panchsheel Park, New Delhi 110 017, India

First published by Penguin Books Australia Ltd 1997
This second edition published 1999

10 9 8 7 6 5 4 3 2 1

Design by Cathy Larsen, Penguin Design Studio
Typeset in 9/12pt Stone Sans by Post Pre-press Group, Brisbane
Printed in Australia by Australian Print Group, Maryborough, Victoria

National Library of Australia
Cataloguing-in-Publication data

Nicholson, Margaret, 1931– .
    The pocket Aussie fact book.

    2nd ed.
    Bibliography.
    ISBN 0 14 028789 2.

    1. Australia – Miscellanea. I. Title.

994

www.penguin.com.au

Contents

Preface

Most people are interested in knowing what makes a country 'tick'. Most are not greatly concerned with the past but are vitally aware of forces shaping their lives today. However, to discover these forces it is necessary to look back at events in our history and to people who have helped mould them – people who, at the time, had little knowledge that they were part of the grand plan which has shaped our nation.

I have always considered myself fortunate to be an Australian. I think Australia is one of the most wonderful places on earth. Researching Australian facts gives me great pleasure and I hope that this little book may help you understand a little more about what makes this country so exciting.

History

The Australian Aborigines existed in almost total isolation for over 60 000 years. They had no written history, but investigation of Dreamtime stories, cave paintings and etchings reveals a culture remarkable in its complexity and richness. Strong spiritual ties link them to the land which influences their lives from birth to death. Each person embraces a plant or animal 'totem' with specific rules of behaviour.

Before white settlement, more than 600 tribes based their lives on hunting, fishing and seed gathering. Evidence suggests that ground-edged tools were used by Aborigines 10 000 years before they were used in Europe.

The colonisation of the land from 1788 by white settlers almost destroyed this fragile society and many Aborigines were separated from their spiritual place and became dispossessed.

In 1850 segregation laws were passed to protect the Aborigines from poverty by confining them to missions or reserves. On the fringe of white society, problems in health, housing and education became endemic.

In the 1950s attitudes began to change. Aborigines became more aware of their identity and white society recognised the appalling treatment they had suffered. Health services were overhauled and housing and education services became a national priority. Even so, in 1999 enormous problems still remain.

Aborigines were granted the vote in 1962 and were included in the census for the first time in 1967. It was not until 1992, when the High Court of Australia handed down the landmark *Mabo* judgement, that Aborigines who could prove unbroken occupancy of land could lodge a claim to that land. Then followed the *Wik* decision of 1996, which held that the grant of pastoral leases did not necessarily extinguish native title and that in some circumstances the two could coexist. In 1998, the Federal Court of Australia ruled that native title can exist over coastal waters. In the *Yorta Yorta* native title claim the Federal Court ruled that, in some cases, 'the tide of history can wash away entitlement'.

Historical notes
'Terra Australis incognita' was inhabited by its Aboriginal people.

1606	Willem Jansz lands on west coast of Cape York, Queensland.
1616	Dirk Hartog lands on the island off the west coast of Australia.
1642	Abel Tasman discovers Van Diemen's Land (Tasmania).
1770	Captain James Cook lands at Botany Bay. He names eastern coastline 'New South Wales' for Britain.
1788	Beginning of European settlement as a penal colony. Arrival of Governor Arthur Phillip and First Fleet at Botany Bay on 18 January then at Port Jackson on 26 January. Phillip formally takes possession of the eastern part of the continent including Tasmania.
1793	First free settlers arrive.
1796	Discovery of coal at mouth of Hunter River (Newcastle), New South Wales.
1797	Introduction of merino sheep by John Macarthur.
1798	George Bass and Matthew Flinders circumnavigate Van Diemen's Land in the *Norfolk*.
1802	Discovery of Port Phillip (Victoria) and Port Bowen (Queensland) by Lieutenant John Murray. Matthew Flinders discovers St Vincent Gulf and Spencer Gulf, South Australia.
1804	Lieutenant David Collins establishes a settlement at Hobart, Tasmania.

1807	First shipment of saleable wool to England.
1808	The Rum Rebellion. Deposition of Governor William Bligh.
1813	Crossing of Blue Mountains by Gregory Blaxland, William Charles Wentworth and William Lawson.
1814	Matthew Flinders suggests the name 'Australia' instead of New Holland.
1817	The first bank, Bank of New South Wales (now Westpac) is established.
1819	Lieutenant Phillip King discovers Port Essington, Northern Territory.
1822	Establishment of penal settlement at Macquarie Harbour, Van Diemen's Land.
1823	Brisbane River discovered by John Oxley and three convicts.
1825	Separation of the administration of Van Diemen's Land from New South Wales. Establishment of settlement at Brisbane.
1828	First census taken: 36 000 convicts and free settlers, 2549 military personnel; Aborigines not counted.
1829	First settlement at Swan River, Western Australia. Perth founded.
1834	First settlement at Twofold Bay, New South Wales. Henty brothers form settlement at Portland (Victoria).

1835	Foundation of Melbourne planned by Sir Richard Bourke.
1836	Settlement at Adelaide under Governor Sir John Hindmarsh.
1838	Captain James Bremer establishes Port Essington, Northern Territory.
1839	Area around where Darwin now stands discovered by crew of the *Beagle*.
1840	Transportation of convicts to New South Wales abolished.
1841	New Zealand proclaimed a separate colony.
1842	First elected council in New South Wales.
1847	Melbourne proclaimed a city.
1850	Sydney University founded. Representative government granted to Port Phillip, Van Diemen's Land and South Australia.
1851	Gold discovered in New South Wales by Edward Hargraves. The Port Phillip district becomes a separate colony named Victoria.
1852	Transportation of convicts to Van Diemen's Land and Norfolk Island abolished.
1854	Eureka Stockade riot at Ballarat (Victoria) sparked by gold-miners' objections to high mining licence fees.
1855	Van Diemen's Land renamed Tasmania after its discoverer, Abel Tasman. Responsible government

	granted to New South Wales, Victoria and Tasmania.
1856	Responsible government granted to South Australia.
1857	Adult males granted the right to vote in Victoria.
1858	Adult males granted the right to vote in New South Wales.
1859	Queensland proclaimed a separate colony.
1861	Burke & Wills die while trying to reach Gulf of Carpentaria.
1863	Northern Territory comes under the jurisdiction of South Australia. Gold discovered at Kalgoorlie, Western Australia.
1868	Last transport bringing convicts to Australia lands in Fremantle, Western Australia.
1869	Darwin becomes a permanent settlement.
1872	Transcontinental telegraph completed. First cable message from Sydney to London.
1876	Death of Truganini, last full-blooded Tasmanian Aborigine.
1878	First telephone in Australia.
1880	Ned Kelly, bushranger and rebel, captured.
1883	Silver discovered at Broken Hill, New South Wales.
1885	Australians go to war for first time as New South Wales contingent sent to Sudan, Africa. BHP company floated.

1890	John Forrest becomes Western Australia's first premier.
1899	Sir Henry Parkes delivers 'Tenterfield Address' on federation.
1900	Australia announces its intention of becoming independent from Great Britain.
1901	The Commonwealth of Australia is proclaimed on 1 January. First federal election held. Census gives population as 3 773 801 whites. Aborigines not counted.
1902	Women granted the right to vote in federal elections.
1908	Canberra chosen as site for national capital.
1910	First Commonwealth banknotes issued.
1911	Douglas Mawson leads expedition to Antarctic.
1913	First Commonwealth postage stamps issued.
1914	World War I declared and Australian and New Zealand Army Corps (ANZAC) formed.
1915	ANZAC troops land at Gallipoli on 25 April; evacuated 18 December.
1917	Completion of transcontinental railway.
1918	First wireless message from London to Sydney. Australia House in London opened by George V.
1919	Return of Australian troops from Europe. Ross and Keith Smith make the first flight from England to Australia.

1920	Queensland and Northern Territory Aerial Services (QANTAS) formed by Hudson Fysh. White population now 5 411 300.
1922	Queensland the first state to abolish the death penalty.
1923	Construction of Sydney Harbour Bridge commences.
1927	Seat of government moved from Melbourne to Canberra.
1928	Kingsford Smith flies from America to Australia in *Southern Cross*. Flying doctor service begins. First traffic lights installed in Melbourne.
1929	Beginning of Depression. Fall in exports. Commonwealth government mobilises gold reserves.
1932	Sydney Harbour Bridge opened. Lang government in New South Wales dismissed.
1935	Kingsford Smith lost without trace near the Bay of Bengal. Ansett Airways set up by Reginald Ansett.
1936	Hume Reservoir completed.
1940	20 000 Australian troops embark for service overseas in World War II. Introduction of food, petrol and clothing rationing.
1941	Sinking of HMAS *Sydney* and HMAS *Canberra*. Australian troops besieged at Tobruk.
1942	Darwin and Katherine bombed. Japanese midget submarines in Sydney Harbour.

1943	Industrial conscription introduced.
1944	Pay-as-you-earn (PAYE) taxation introduced. Japanese prisoners of war attempt mass break-out at Cowra, New South Wales – 234 killed.
1946	United Nations grants trusteeship of New Guinea to Australia.
1947	Commonwealth Arbitration Commission established. Immigration program begun.
1948	40-hour week introduced. General Motors-Holden produces first Holden car. Food and clothing rationing ends.
1949	The right to vote granted to some Aborigines. Snowy Mountains hydro-electric scheme commenced. Robert Menzies becomes Prime Minister (Liberal Party).
1950	Petrol rationing ends. Australian troops join UN forces in Korea.
1951	ANZUS Treaty signed by Australia, New Zealand and USA against aggression in the Pacific.
1952	Uranium discovered at Rum Jungle, Northern Territory.
1953	Atomic Energy Commission established. Television Bill passed. Atomic weapons tested by Great Britain at Woomera, South Australia. South-East Asia Treaty Organisation (SEATO) founded.
1954	Queen Elizabeth II makes the first visit to Australia

by a reigning monarch. Troops withdrawn from Korea. 'Petrov Affair': accusations of communist espionage in Department of External Affairs.

1956   Olympic Games held in Melbourne.

1958   The first nuclear reactor opened at Lucas Heights, Sydney.

1960   Aborigines granted citizenship and therefore entitlement to social service benefits. Reserve Bank established.

1961   Huge iron-ore deposits found at Pilbara, Western Australia.

1962   Standard-gauge railway opened between Brisbane, Sydney and Melbourne. Aborigines granted the vote. USA granted permission to build communication base at Exmouth, Western Australia and space tracking station at Tidbinbilla, near Canberra.

1964   HMAS *Voyager* collides with HMAS *Melbourne* – 82 die.

1965   Australian infantry battalion sent to Vietnam. Australia imposes economic sanctions against Rhodesia.

1966   Decimal currency introduced on 14 February. Aborigines appeal to the UN for human rights. Sir Robert Menzies retires as prime minister. Metric system of weights and measures phased in.

1967   Prime Minister Harold Holt disappears at Portsea, Victoria. Aborigines included in census for the first time. Ronald Ryan hanged, the last person to be hanged in Australia.

1968   First Australian heart transplant performed. John Gorton becomes leader of the Liberal Party and prime minister.

1969   HMAS *Melbourne* collides with USS *Frank E Evans* with the loss of 74 lives. Poseidon company announces a nickel discovery and share prices soar. Bob Hawke elected president of the Australian Council of Trade Unions (ACTU). Equal pay for work of equal value granted to women.

1970   Demonstrations against Australian and US involvement in Vietnam. Tullamarine Airport in Melbourne opened.

1971   Australia ends fighting role in Vietnam. Lake Pedder in Tasmania flooded as part of hydroelectric scheme.

1972   Australian Labor Party victory under Gough Whitlam. Troops withdrawn from Vietnam. Formal ending of White Australia immigration policy.

1973   18-year-olds allowed to vote in federal elections.

1974   Cyclone Tracy hits Darwin on Christmas Day. Bankcard introduced.

1975   Whitlam government dismissed by Governor-

General, Sir John Kerr. Liberal – Country Party coalition wins election under Malcolm Fraser. Papua New Guinea becomes independent. No-fault divorce introduced.

1978   Northern Territory becomes responsible for its own administration.

1979   Aboriginal Land Trust gains title to 144 properties formerly Aboriginal reserves.

1980   Baby Azaria Chamberlain allegedly taken by a dingo at Ayers Rock.

1982   New South Wales introduces random breath testing of drivers. Lindy Chamberlain found guilty of the murder of her daughter, Azaria.

1983   Labor Party gain government under Bob Hawke. *Australia II* wins America Cup.

1984   World's first test-tube quads born in Melbourne.

1985   Federal government allows the application for a banking licence from sixteen foreign banks.

1986   A fringe benefits tax is introduced. Bombing of Russell St police headquarters.

1987   Share market collapses. Seven people killed in the Hoddle St Massacre, Melbourne.

1988   Australia celebrates bicentenary of white settlement. Queen opens new Parliament House. Charges against Lindy Chamberlain and her husband Michael are quashed.

1989   Newcastle suffers devastating earthquake leaving twelve dead. Australian cricket team brings home the Ashes for the first time in 34 years.

1990   Corporate failures continue as worst depression for 40 years takes hold.

1991   Government bans mining of uranium at Coronation Hill, Kakadu. Heart transplant pioneer Dr Victor Chang murdered. Nine die in massacre in Strathfield Shopping Plaza. Paul Keating takes over from Bob Hawke as prime minister.

1992   1c and 2c coins phased out. Plastic $5 note introduced. Unemployment reaches 11.3%. Anglican Synod allows ordination of women priests. Sydney Harbour tunnel opens.

1993   ALP wins record fifth successive term. Sydney wins the right to host the 2000 Olympics.

1994   Plastic $10 and $20 notes introduced. Drought blankets eastern Australia. Bodies of seven murdered backpackers found in the Belanglo State Forest.

1995   Rugby Super League controversy rages. Balance of payments historically high. John Howard takes over as Liberal Party leader. Plastic $50 note introduced.

1996   Landslide victory to Liberals, and John Howard becomes prime minister. Massacre at Port Arthur in Tasmania, 35 dead. Gun Summit bans all automatic and some semi-automatic weapons. Euthanasia legalised in Northern Territory. 18 soldiers die in Blackhawk helicopter crash in Queensland. Super League wins Federal Court appeal allowing alternative Rugby League competitions. Backpacker murderer, Ivan Milat, convicted. Martin Bryant given 35 life sentences for the massacre at Port Arthur.

1997   Wood Royal Commission into corruption foreshadows sweeping changes in NSW. Federal Senate overrides NT euthanasia legislation. BHP announces withdrawal of steel-making in Newcastle. Four Australians dead after Maccabiah Games in Israel. 18 killed in Thredbo landslide in NSW – Stuart Diver sole survivor.

1998   Constitutional Convention results in promise of Republic referendum. Michael Hutchence, lead singer of INXS, dies tragically. Two American tourists disappear after being abandoned on Great Barrier Reef cruise. Four sailors perish in fire aboard HMAS *Westralia*. Landmark Federal Court ruling that native title can exist over coastal waters. Historic ruling in favour of native claims over large tracts of land in the Kimberley, WA. Five volunteers die in Victorian bushfires.

Federal Court rules that 'the tide of history can wash away entitlements' in native title claim. Prolonged dispute on waterfront results in a compromise. Mining in Kakadu continues despite World Heritage listing. Sydney water contamination scare. Seven die in disastrous Sydney-to-Hobart yacht race.

1999   Salt Lake City Olympic bid scandal erupts, sending shock waves through AOC. Unemployment hits 7.5% – the lowest for decades. Controversy over removal of Aboriginal embassy from the lawns of old Parliament House after 15 years' residency. Kurdish assault on Greek consulates in Sydney and Melbourne after global mobilisation of Kurds. Australia rocked by numerous violent deaths and assaults in the space of five February days. Australian researchers discover that the hormone CRH is the link which causes some premature births.

Australia in its region

Australia Overview

Location

Australia consists of two land masses: mainland Australia and Tasmania. It lies on and extends south from the Tropic of Capricorn in the southern hemisphere between latitudes 10°41' and 43°39'S and longitudes 113°9' and 153°39'E. It is bounded by the Pacific Ocean to the east, the Indian Ocean to the west, the Arafura Sea to the north and the Southern Ocean to the south. The nearest neighbour is Papua New Guinea, 200 km north. Timor is 640 km to the north-west, New Zealand is 1920 km east, and Antarctica is 2000 km due south.

Area

The area of Australia is 7 682 300 square km. Australia is about the size of the mainland states of the United States, excluding Alaska, and approximately 24 times the size of the British Isles.

Distances

Mainland east-west, 3983 km; north-south, 3138 km. Coastline including Tasmania and off-shore islands, 36 735 km.

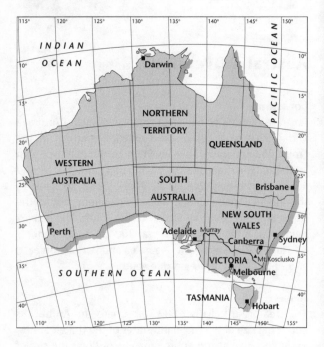

Landform

Australia is one of the oldest continents and, because of the effects of 250 million years of erosion, it has become the flattest land mass on earth. It is considered to be the most stable land mass in the world being free of any major mountain-building events for the past 80 million years. But Australia has a wide variety of landforms – mostly consisting of vast ancient crystal blocks. The lowest elevation is Lake Eyre (South Australia), which is 16 metres below sea level, and the highest peak is Mt Kosciusko, which is 2228 metres above sea level.

Climate

There are generally no great extremes of climate but it is varied because of the size of the continent. The summer temperature range is from 23–26°C north of the Tropic of Capricorn to 38°C in the arid plateaus and deserts of the interior. The southern areas are more temperate although subject to wide variations – high rainfall, extreme heat and irregular flooding and drought. Australia is considered to be one of the driest continents on earth.

Time zones

There are three time zones within the Australian continent. The eastern states – Queensland, New South Wales, Tasmania and Victoria – are 30 minutes ahead of South

Rainfall in mm
Temperature in deg. Celsius

Darwin

Broome

Carnarvon

Uluru
(Ayers Rock)

Perth

Kalgoorlie

20

Cairns

Townsville

Mt. Isa

Alice Springs

Rockhampton

Broken Hill

Brisbane

Adelaide

Canberra

Sydney

Melbourne

Hobart

21

Australia and the Northern Territory (including Broken Hill), and two hours ahead of Western Australia.

Daylight saving

New South Wales, Victoria and Tasmania follow Eastern Summer Time but Queensland has decided not to adopt this practice. South Australia follows South Australian Summer Time, which also covers the Northern Territory. This period usually falls between November and February but can extend for up to two weeks on either side. Tasmania has extended daylight saving to six months from early October to late March.

Population

The Australian population by the year 2000 is estimated to reach 19.2 million. Because of the arid interior, most people live around the coastline. Although it is considered to have one of the highest degrees of urban concentration in the world, the density of population is low by international standards, with an average of two persons per square km. Many of its people came to Australia from elsewhere – one in every four persons is either a first- or second-generation settler.

Population distribution

Sydney	3 986 723
Melbourne	3 371 308
Brisbane	1 574 615
Perth	1 341 914
Adelaide	1 088 349
Canberra	308 086
Hobart	194 974
Darwin	86 576

Flags

The Australian Blue Ensign was proclaimed the national flag in 1951. This is a plain blue flag with the Union Jack in the upper corner of the hoist together with the seven-pointed Commonwealth star beneath. It also contains the five-starred Southern Cross.

The state flags are based on the plain Blue Ensign with the particular badge of each state added. The Northern Territory flag is based on colours found in desert regions with the Territory's badge added.

Coat of arms

The present coat of arms was granted in 1912 by King George V. It consists of a shield composed of six parts, each containing one of the state badges. These are surrounded by an ermine border, signifying the federation of the states into the Commonwealth. The shield is supported by two Australian animals, the kangaroo and the emu, standing on ornamental rests, behind which are small branches of wattle. The crest consists of the seven-pointed Commonwealth gold star, a symbol of national unity. At the base of the shield is a scroll on which is printed the word 'Australia'.

Emblems

The national floral emblem is the golden wattle and the national animal emblem is the kangaroo.

Anthems

The royal anthem, 'God Save the Queen', is used in the presence of Her Majesty the Queen or a member of the royal family.

The vice-regal salute which consists of the first four and last four bars of the national anthem 'Advance Australia

Fair' is used in the presence of the governor-general.

The national anthem 'Advance Australia Fair' is used on all other ceremonial occasions.

Advance Australia Fair

Australians all let us rejoice,
For we are young and free,
We've golden soil and wealth for toil;
Our home is girt by sea;
Our land abounds in nature's gifts
Of beauty rich and rare;
In history's page, let every stage
Advance Australia Fair.

Beneath our radiant Southern Cross,
We'll toil with hearts and hands;
To make this Commonwealth of ours
Renowned of all the lands;
For those who've come across the seas
We've boundless plains to share;
With courage let us all combine
To Advance Australia Fair.
In joyful strains then let us sing,
Advance Australia Fair.

Public holidays & special days

January

1	New Year's Day
26	Australia Day

March

first Monday	Labour Day (WA)
first Monday	8-hour Day (Tas)
second Monday	Labour Day (Vic)
third Monday	Labour Day (ACT)

April

first full moon	Easter (Good Friday to Easter Monday;
after equinox	Easter Tuesday holiday in some states)
25	Anzac Day

May

first Monday	Labour Day (Qld)
first Monday	May Day (NT)

June

second Monday	Queen's Birthday (not WA)

August

1	Wattle Day (some states)
first Monday	Bank Holiday (NSW)

September	
1	Wattle Day (some states)

October	
first Monday	Labour Day (NSW and ACT)
6	Queen's Birthday (WA)
second Monday	Labour Day (SA)

November	
first Tuesday	Melbourne Cup Day (Melbourne metro only)
11	Remembrance Day

December	
25	Christmas Day
26	Boxing Day (not SA)
28	Proclamation Day (SA)

Government

Australia's official name is the Commonwealth of Australia. Its form of government is a constitutional monarchy. The head of state is Queen Elizabeth II of the United Kingdom of Great Britain and Northern Ireland and also Queen of Australia. She is represented in Australia by the governor-general. The head of government is the prime minister, leader of the party or coalition of parties holding a majority in federal parliament.

Australia is an independent self-governing member of the British Commonwealth of Nations and a foundation member of the United Nations. It is in alliance with the United States of America and New Zealand in the ANZUS pact and a member of the South-East Asia Treaty Organisation (SEATO).

Australia is a federation of six states with two internal federal territories (Australian Capital Territory and Northern

Territory) and a number of external territories under its control – Norfolk Island, Cocos Island, Christmas Island, Lord Howe Island, Macquarie Island, and Australian Antarctica between longitudes 45° and 160°.

Federal government

The Australian federal parliament is based on the British Westminster system with a prime minister and cabinet. It is responsible for matters of national importance – defence, external affairs, customs and excise, communications, foreign trade, social services, treasury and immigration. It also shares mutual responsibilities with the state legislatures for education, agriculture, energy services, health and law enforcement.

There are two houses in the federal parliament – the House of Representatives (lower house) and the Senate (upper house).

House of Representatives

This is often called the people's house as the 148 members are voted in directly by the people of Australia with each member representing about 70 000 voters. The House consists of government and opposition members (MPs) voted in at the most recent general election. It sits for 70 to 80 days each year and is limited to a three-year period. However it may be dissolved sooner by the governor-general on the advice of the prime minister. Its main function is to debate and discuss bills which are proposed new laws. The debates within the House are regulated by the Speaker who is chosen from among the governing party. The members sit on opposing sides of the House – the government to the right of the Speaker and the opposition to the left. Independents sit in the cross-benches facing the Speaker.

The Senate

This is virtually a house of review where the procedures are designed to allow debate on the merits or defects of any bill passed by the House of Representatives. The Senate can request amendments to, and can reject, any bill. In 1999 there were 76 senators, 12 from each state and 2 from each internal territory. Each senator represents the whole state, not just a small area. Senators from states are elected for a six-year period. Every three years half the senators retire but may stand for re-election. Senators from the territories are elected for three years.

The Ministry

This consists of members of the government who are responsible for a particular area of policy. Most ministers are members of the House of Representatives and a few are from the Senate. They have specific departments of the public service to help them administer their portfolios. The prime minister is, by convention, always a member of the House of Representatives. Ministers and other leading members of the government are called frontbenchers because they sit on the front benches in the parliament. Other members are called backbenchers.

The Opposition forms a shadow government with members in the same positions as the government.

Cabinet

This is an inner council and consists of the leading figures (those with senior portfolios) of the government and the Senate with the prime minister as chairman. Junior ministers attend cabinet meetings only when matters affecting their departments are being discussed.

The executive council

It advises the governor-general of major political decisions affecting the nation which have been made by the Cabinet.

The governor-general

He is the Queen's representative in the Australian parliament and is appointed by the Queen on the advice of the prime minister. All laws made by parliament finally depend on his assent. This should be a formality.

Prime ministers

Sir Edmund Barton	1 Jan 1901 – 24 Sep 1903
Alfred Deakin	24 Sep 1903 – 27 Apr 1904
John Christian Watson	27 Apr 1904 – 18 Aug 1904
George Reid	18 Aug 1904 – 5 Jul 1905
Alfred Deakin	5 Jul 1905 – 13 Nov 1908
Andrew Fisher	13 Nov 1908 – 2 Jun 1909
Alfred Deakin	2 Jun 1909 – 29 Apr 1910
Andrew Fisher	29 Apr 1910 – 24 Jun 1913
Sir Joseph Cook	24 Jun 1913 – 17 Sep 1914
Andrew Fisher	17 Sep 1914 – 27 Oct 1915
William Morris Hughes	27 Oct 1915 – 9 Feb 1922
Stanley Melbourne Bruce	9 Feb 1922 – 22 Oct 1929
James Henry Scullin	22 Oct 1929 – 6 Jan 1932
Joseph Aloysius Lyons	6 Jan 1932 – 7 Apr 1939
Sir Earle Page	7 Apr 1939 – 26 Apr 1939
Sir Robert Gordon Menzies	26 Apr 1939 – 29 Aug 1941
Sir Arthur W. Fadden	29 Aug 1941 – 7 Oct 1941
John Curtin	7 Oct 1941 – 5 Jul 1945
Francis Michael Forde	6 Jul 1945 – 13 Jul 1945
Joseph Benedict Chifley	13 Jul 1945 – 19 Dec 1949
Sir Robert Gordon Menzies	19 Dec 1949 – 26 Jan 1966
Harold Edward Holt	26 Jan 1966 – 19 Dec 1967
Sir John McEwen	19 Dec 1967 – 10 Jan 1968
Sir John Grey Gorton	10 Jan 1968 – 10 Mar 1971

Sir William McMahon	10 Mar 1971 – 8 Dec 1972
Edward Gough Whitlam	8 Dec 1972 – 11 Nov 1975
John Malcolm Fraser	11 Nov 1975 – 5 Mar 1983
Robert James Lee Hawke	5 Mar 1983 – 19 Dec 1991
Paul John Keating	19 Dec 1991 – 2 Mar 1996
John Winston Howard	2 Mar 1996 –

Voting

All Australian citizens over the age of 18 are eligible to vote. Voting is compulsory for everyone except Aborigines. Aborigines may choose whether or not to register; if they register, they must vote. Compulsory preferential voting is the most common system used in Australia. In voting for the House of Representatives one candidate only from any one party is selected to represent each electorate. The voter must vote for all the candidates in order of preference. If no candidate receives an absolute majority, then there is a distribution of preference votes.

The number of members of the House of Representatives depends on the population of each state. In 1999 there were 148 members, 50 for New South Wales, 37 for Victoria, 27 for Queensland, 12 for South Australia, 5 for Tasmania, 14 for Western Australia, 2 for the Australian Capital Territory and 1 for the Northern Territory.

Proportional representation is the other major electoral

system in Australia. It is used in the Senate and in some state elections. Each senator represents a whole state; as the electorate is so large, more than one candidate is elected for each state. In 1999 there were 76 senators, 12 for each state and 2 for each territory.

State government

State governments run along the same lines as the federal government, each having a premier as leader, a cabinet and ministry, and an opposition. State parliaments deal with state affairs such as housing, trade, education, industry and law enforcement as well as sharing mutual responsibilities with the federal parliament.

Five states have both a lower house or Legislative Assembly (House of Assembly in South Australia and Tasmania) and upper house or Legislative Council. Queensland opted to have only one house, a Legislative Assembly. The Northern Territory and Australian Capital Territory each have a Legislative Assembly.

Local government

The Local Government Act of 1919 gave power to areas as small as cities, municipalities and shires, to provide a more satisfactory system of government within the local area. The mayor or president is leader of a number of councillors who are elected by the ratepayers of the area.

The principal officer is a general manager who is responsible for the overall administration and is answerable to council. Directors or managers are in charge of various departments, such as health and development, planning, engineering and community affairs, and are answerable to the general manager. Australia has 900 bodies at local government level.

Judicial system

There are three types of courts at state level. Australia has 175 **local courts** (previously called Courts of Petty Sessions) which deal with 98% of all cases. They mostly deal with less serious offences and preliminary enquiries into major crimes. Plaintiffs can appeal to the **District (County) Court** where a judge hears civil cases and appeals. A judge and jury hears criminal cases and appeals. The **Supreme Court** deals with special areas such as equity, probate and administrative law. Plaintiffs can appeal to the Federal Court of Australia and the High Court of Australia.

There are three federal courts. The **High Court** has jurisdiction over matters where the Commonwealth is a party. It also acts as a final court of appeal for cases from elsewhere in the system. The **Federal Court** deals with industrial matters, bankruptcy, trade practices and administrative review. The **Family Court** deals with marriage, divorce and custody and property settlement after a divorce.

Economy

The Australian economy follows the system of free enterprise and orderly marketing of products. In 1991 the tariff barrier was eased by the government.

The federal and state governments have separate areas of responsibility for raising and spending revenue. The financial year runs from 1 July to 30 June.

Federal government income

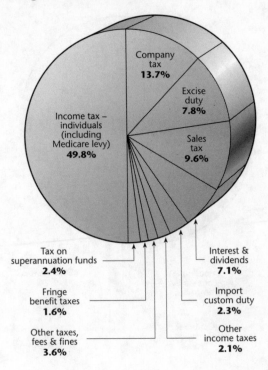

Company tax
13.7%

Excise duty
7.8%

Sales tax
9.6%

Income tax –
individuals
(including
Medicare levy)
49.8%

Tax on
superannuation funds
2.4%

Fringe
benefit taxes
1.6%

Other taxes,
fees & fines
3.6%

Interest &
dividends
7.1%

Import
custom duty
2.3%

Other
income taxes
2.1%

Federal government expenditure

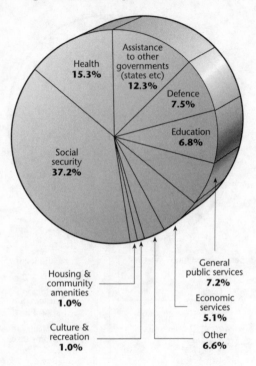

Health **15.3%**

Assistance to other governments (states etc) **12.3%**

Defence **7.5%**

Education **6.8%**

Social security **37.2%**

Housing & community amenities **1.0%**

Culture & recreation **1.0%**

General public services **7.2%**

Economic services **5.1%**

Other **6.6%**

State government income

tax revenue	51.8%
special Commonwealth government grants and payments	39.6%
interest from public utilities and other income	8.6%

State government expenditure

public health	23.1%
education	22.9%
general public services	15.8%
transport	12.2%
law and order	8.8%
social and community services	7.2%
housing and water	4.5%
agriculture, mining and forestry	2.8%
recreation and cultural	2.7%

Trade

Australia trades with two main groups of countries: the European Union (EU), which consists of countries with common economic policies (such as France, Germany, Italy, Sweden and the UK); and the Asia-Pacific Economic Cooperation group (APEC), which includes Canada, USA, China, Japan, Indonesia, New Zealand, Singapore and Taiwan.

Imports

Australia imports mostly manufactured goods, machinery, transport equipment and chemicals totalling about $90.68 billion per year. Main trading areas are:

Import value in $billions	
APEC	61.85
EU	21.83
Other	7.00

Exports

Australia exports mostly minerals, meat, cereals, textiles and manufactured goods totalling about $87.76 billion per year. Main trading areas are:

Export value in $billions	
APEC	63.60
EU	10.23
Other	13.93

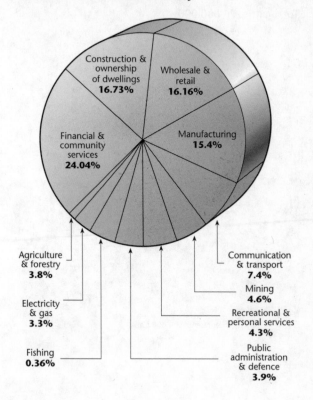

Overview of Australian industry

Construction & ownership of dwellings **16.73%**

Wholesale & retail **16.16%**

Manufacturing **15.4%**

Financial & community services **24.04%**

Agriculture & forestry **3.8%**

Electricity & gas **3.3%**

Fishing **0.36%**

Communication & transport **7.4%**

Mining **4.6%**

Recreational & personal services **4.3%**

Public administration & defence **3.9%**

Australian agriculture (1998)
Total cattle 26 800 000

Represents 500 000 Cattle

Total sheep 119 600 000
Wool production 730 000 tonnes

⌒ Represents 500 000 Sheep

Total wheat 9 243 000 hectares; 16 566 000 tonnes
Coarse grain 6 879 000 hectares; 13 496 000 tonnes

◊ Represents 50 000 hectares wheat

◆ Represents 50 000 hectares coarse grain

Sugar cane 377 000 hectares (est.); 35 889 000 tonnes
Fruit and vines 195 000 hectares (est.); 2 376 000 tonnes
Cotton 315 000 hectares; 923 000 tonnes

♀ Represents 3000 hectares cotton
❙ Represents 3000 hectares sugar cane
○ Represents 3000 hectares fruit and vines

Currency

Decimal currency was introduced on 14 February 1966, the dollar (A$) being the unit of currency and consisting of 100 cents (¢).

Coins

The coins are: 5¢, 10¢, 20¢, 50¢, $1 and $2. All coins display an image of Queen Elizabeth II on the obverse side and on the reverse side are as follows:

The **5¢** coin shows the echidna or spiny anteater, one of the only two egg-laying mammals in the world.

The **10¢** coin shows a male lyrebird dancing, its magnificent tail spread and thrown forward over its head.

The **20¢** coin shows the platypus – the only other egg-laying mammal in the world.

The **50¢** coin shows the Commonwealth of Australia's coat of arms. This coin is sometimes minted with special designs for commemorative purposes.

The **$1** coin shows the kangaroo. It also has interrupted milling on the edge to assist visually impaired people.

The **$2** coin shows an Aborigine against a background of the Southern Cross.

Notes

There are five notes ($5, $10, $20, $50, $100), each a different colour and increasing in size with value. All depict personalities and themes of Australian historical interest.

They are all polymer (plastic) which allows the incorporation of sophisticated security features (most notably the clear window which can include printing and embossing). The plastic notes were first introduced in 1992.

The **$5** note features the portrait of Queen Elizabeth II and gum leaves on the front, and Parliament House, Canberra, landscape plans and geometric shapes on the back. A gum flower can be seen in the clear window.

The **$10** note features the portrait of A. B. (Banjo) Paterson, surrounded by microprinted excerpts from his famous poem 'The Man from Snowy River' on the front. On the back is the portrait of poet and champion of the oppressed, Dame Mary Gilmore, surrounded by micro-printed excerpts from her poem 'No Foe Shall Gather Our Harvest', with a bullock team in the background. The clear window has a windmill printed on it, along with embossed wave patterns.

The **$20** note features the portrait of Mary Reibey, who came to the colony as a convict, and later became a respected businesswoman with interests in property and shipping. The reverse side commemorates the work of Reverend John Flynn, founder of the world-acclaimed Royal Flying Doctor Service. The clear window has a stylised compass printed in it, along with embossing of the number '20'.

The **$50** note features the portrait of David Unaipon, an inventor and Australia's first published Aboriginal author on the front, and Edith Cowan, a social worker and Australia's first female parliamentarian on the back. The clear window has a stylised version of the Southern Cross printed on it, along with embossing of the number '50'.

The **$100** note features a portrait of Dame Nellie Melba, one of Australia's best-known opera singers, and Sir John Monash, a soldier, engineer and administrator who is acknowledged for his outstanding leadership qualities in both military and civilian life. The clear window has a stylised image of a lyrebird and an embossed '100'.

State by State

Australian Capital Territory

Two areas transferred to the Commonwealth of Australia by the state of New South Wales originally made up the Australian Capital Territory (ACT). In 1908 the larger area around Canberra was chosen for the federal capital site, and in 1915 the smaller area of Jervis Bay on the New South Wales coast was transferred to the Commonwealth of Australia for development as a port. In 1993, after the formation of the ACT Legislative Assembly, the area around

Canberra was deemed the ACT and Jervis Bay remained Commonwealth territory.

Location

The greater part of the ACT is in south-eastern New South Wales, west of the Great Dividing Range. The smaller Jervis Bay area is on the New South Wales southern coast.

Area

The area around Canberra is 2400 square km; Jervis Bay consists of 73 square km.

Landform

Rolling plains and grasslands.

Population

308 411, mostly residents of Canberra (308 086).

Climate

Mainly temperate: cold nights and cool to very cold days in winter, warm to hot days and cool nights in summer. Slightly humid in coastal areas. Average daily hours of sunshine, 7.2.

Administrative centre

Canberra is situated at the northern end of the ACT. It has an area of 805 square km and a population of 298 425, of which 28% are public servants.

Industry

In the ACT, government administration, health and cultural services account for 95% of production, agriculture 2.4% and mining 2.1%.

Main attractions

Parliament House, Lake Burley Griffin, National Gallery of Australia, High Court of Australia, Captain Cook Memorial Water Jet, Red Hill, Black Mountain, Telstra Tower, American War Memorial, Australian War Memorial, foreign legations, Yarralumla (governor-general's residence), Vietnam War Memorial.

Major festivals

February	Royal Canberra Show
March	Canberra Festival
September	Floriade
October	Oktoberfest

DID YOU KNOW?
Walter Burley Griffin, an American landscape architect, came to Australia in 1913, after winning a worldwide competition for a design for Australia's new capital city, Canberra. He designed the city to follow the contours of the land and the buildings to blend into the natural setting.

New South Wales

Location

NSW lies in the south-east of the continent on the Pacific Ocean, with Queensland to the north and Victoria to the south.

Area

It is the fourth-largest state and is 801 600 square km (seven times larger than England).

Landform

Coastal slopes, plateaus and river flats are bounded by the Great Dividing Range, which runs north and south. West of the Dividing Range are rolling plains which deteriorate into semiarid desert.

Population

6 341 594 with the majority living in the three main cities – Sydney, Newcastle and Wollongong. Over half the state's population lives in Sydney.

Climate

Temperate and slightly humid in coastal areas with the deserts of the interior experiencing cold nights and hot days. Irregular floods and droughts occur. Average daily hours of sunshine 6.7.

State capital

Sydney is built on Port Jackson, a sea inlet on the Pacific Ocean. The city has an area of 12 407 square km (including Penrith and Gosford), and a population of 3 986 723.

Largest cities

Sydney	3 986 723
Newcastle-Hunter	567 302
Wollongong-Illawarra	380 660
Wagga Wagga	56 566
Albury	50 192
Tamworth	35 326
Broken Hill	21 297

Industry

In New South Wales, health, education, cultural and other services, government and utilities account for 70% of the contribution to gross state product, the balance coming from manufacturing 15%, wholesale and retail 14%, with the remainder spread over mining and primary industry.

Chief products

Agriculture: wool, wheat, beef, cotton, mutton, dairy products, fruit, honey, poultry, sugar, timber.
Fishing: many varieties of fish and shellfish.
Manufacturing: agricultural implements, chemicals, clothing, fertiliser, glassware, iron and steel, machinery, motor cars, paper, textiles.
Mining: coal, copper, gold, lead, mineral sands, silver, zinc.

Main attractions

Sydney Harbour Bridge, Opera House, Darling Harbour, Rocks area, Olympic site at Homebush, Blue Mountains, Murrumbidgee irrigation area, Snowy Mountains, national parks, surfing beaches, fishing, wineries.

Flag

The New South Wales flag is based on the Blue Ensign with the state badge superimposed on the right-hand side. The badge consists of a golden lion on a red St George Cross within a white circle.

Coat of Arms

The present coat of arms was approved in 1906 by King Edward VII. It consists of a shield with the red cross of St George supported by a lion and a kangaroo. The motto is, 'Newly risen, how brightly you shine'.

Emblems

Animal: platypus
Floral: waratah
Bird: kookaburra

Major festivals

January	Festival of Sydney
	Tamworth Country Music Festival
February	Sydney Gay & Lesbian Mardi Gras
August	Newcastle Mattara Festival
October	Bathurst 1000 car race

DID YOU KNOW?
Sydney Tower, at Centrepoint, is the highest building in the southern hemisphere, 324.8 metres above sea level.

Victoria

Location

Victoria lies in the south-eastern corner of the continent

Area

It is the smallest state on the mainland and is 227 600 square km in area.

Landform

Mountainous areas in the north-east, and semiarid areas in the north-west. Most land is well suited to farming, and as a result Victoria is often referred to as the 'garden state'.

Population

4 660 885. Victoria is the most densely populated and most highly urbanised of all the states.

Climate

Generally temperate although the climate is subject to wide variation. High rainfall, extremes of summer heat and irregular floods and droughts occur. Average daily hours of sunshine 5.7.

State capital

Melbourne is situated on the Yarra River, on Port Phillip Bay. It has an area of 6109 square km and a population of 3 371 308 (about 70% of the state's population). Melbourne's motto is *Vires acquirit eundo* or 'We gather strength as we grow'.

Largest cities

Melbourne	3 371 308
Geelong and environs	154 500
Ballarat	80 330
Bendigo	75 857
Shepparton	41 910

Industry

In Victoria, health, education, cultural and other services, government and utilities account for 63% of the contribution to gross state product, the balance coming from manufacturing 18%, wholesale and retail 13%, with the remainder spread over mining and primary industry.

Chief products

Agriculture: cattle, forest products, fruit, hay and straw, milk and dairy products, poultry and eggs, sheep, vegetables, wheat, wool.

Manufacturing: building materials, chemical products, clothing, farm machinery, footwear, light engineering, motor vehicles, textiles.

Mining: brown coal, natural gas, oil.

Main attractions

Melbourne Cup (began 1861), Australian Rules Football, National Tennis Centre, Formula One Grand Prix, Phillip Island (penguins), wineries, prospecting, riverboat cruising, surfing, snowfields, national parks, sailing, fishing.

Flag

Victoria was the first state to have its own flag. The flag is made up of the Blue Ensign with the badge of the state which consists of five white stars of the Southern Cross in the fly with a crown above.

Coat of arms

The present coat of arms was granted by Queen Elizabeth II in 1972. It incorporates a shield of five stars representing the constellation of the Southern Cross. On either side stands a female figure, one representing peace and the other prosperity. The motto is 'Peace and prosperity'.

Emblems

Animal: Leadbeater's possum
Floral: pink heath

Major festivals

March	Melbourne Moomba Festival
	Melbourne Formula One Grand Prix
Easter	Stawell Gift foot race
April/May	Bright Autumn Festival
	500cc Motorcycle Grand Prix at Phillip Island
October	Dandenongs Tulip Festival
November	Melbourne Cup

DID YOU KNOW?
The Yarra River, an important waterway and part of Melbourne's water supply, flows 250 km from Mt Baw Baw in the Great Dividing Range, south-west to its estuary in Port Phillip Bay. Baw Baw is an Aboriginal word meaning 'running water'.

Queensland

Location

Queensland lies on the north-east of the continent, bordering the Pacific Ocean to the east, and Torres Strait to the north.

Area

Second-largest state: 1 727 200 square km.

Landform

The north coast is sheltered by islands and the Great Barrier Reef system. Behind the coastal slopes of the Great Dividing Range and river flats, are rolling plains, then the land becomes semiarid desert.

Population

3 456 345, mostly in four coastal areas.

Climate

The climate is mostly tropical with two main seasons – wet and dry. Queensland is known as the 'sunshine state' because of pleasantly warm winters and long hours of sunshine. Average daily hours of sunshine, 7.5.

State capital

Brisbane, situated on the Brisbane River on the east coast. It has an area of 3080 square km and a population of 1 574 615.

Largest cities

Brisbane	1 574 615
Gold Coast and environs	337 406
Townsville	145 099
Cairns and environs	111 916
Rockhampton	64 437
Mackay	63 548
Mt Isa	22 061

Industry

In Queensland, health, education, cultural and other services, government and utilities account for 63% of the contribution to gross state product, the balance coming from manufacturing 12%, wholesale and retail 15%, with the remainder spread over mining and primary industry 5% each.

Chief products

Agriculture: barley, cattle, cotton, fruit, maize, peanuts, pigs, sheep, sugar, tobacco, wheat, wool.
Fishing: many varieties of fish, prawns.
Manufacturing: aerated waters, basic metal products, brick-making, dairy products, electricity generation, meat products, ready-mixed concrete, timber processing.
Mining: bauxite, coal, copper, gold, lead, mineral sands, nickel, salt, tin, uranium, zinc.

Main attractions

The Great Barrier Reef (a complex organic system and one of the greatest biological wonders of the world), Gold Coast, Sunshine Coast, Cape York Peninsula, Indy car race, surf beaches, fishing, tropical islands, prospecting, national parks, rainforests, whale-watching.

Flag

The flag is based on the Blue Ensign with the state badge superimposed on the right-hand side. It has a blue Maltese Cross with the Imperial Crown in the centre. This badge was proclaimed in 1876.

Coat of arms

The present coat of arms was granted by Queen Elizabeth II in 1977. It consists of a shield with pictures representing pastoral, mining and agricultural industries. This is supported by a red deer and the brolga. The motto means 'Bold, aye, but faithful too'.

Emblems

Animal: koala
Floral: Cooktown orchid

Major festivals

June	Brisbane Festival of Creative Arts
September	Mackay's Sugartime Festival
	Toowoomba Carnival of Flowers
October	Cairns Fun in the Sun Festival
	Ipswich Country Music Festival
	Rockhampton Rocktoberfest
December	Woodford Folk Festival

DID YOU KNOW?
The world's largest structure created by living creatures is the Great Barrier Reef. It extends along the Queensland coast for more than 2000 km and covers an area of almost 260 000 square km.

South Australia

Location

South Australia occupies a central position on the southern coastline. Seaward is the Great Australian Bight.

Area

It is the third-largest state and covers one-eighth of the total area of Australia. It is 984 000 square km in area, with a coastline of 3700 km.

Landform

Undulating hills, grasslands and valleys; semiarid to arid deserts in the north.

Population

Sparsely populated with 1 487 294 people mainly concentrated in the south-east corner of the state.

Climate

Mostly a Mediterranean climate, warm to hot in summer and cool in winter. It is the driest state with four-fifths of its total area receiving less than 254 mm of rainfall a year. Average daily hours of sunshine, 6.9.

State capital

Adelaide, situated on the Torrens River in St Vincent Gulf and sheltered by the Mt Lofty Range. The population is 1 088 349 and its area is 1870 square km.

Largest cities and towns

Adelaide	1 088 349
Elizabeth	25 900
Whyalla	24 286
Mt Gambier	23 055
Port Pirie	18 094
Port Augusta	13 995

Industry

In South Australia, health, education, cultural and other services, government and utilities account for 62% of the contribution to gross state product, the balance coming from manufacturing 18%, wholesale and retail 14%, with the remainder spread over mining and primary industry.

Chief products

Agriculture: almonds, barley, beef, dairy products, fruits, vegetables, wheat, wine, wool.

Manufacturing: carriages and wagons, chemical, cotton, electrical goods, iron and steel, machinery, motor cars, pipes.

Mining: barytes, coal, copper, dolomite, gypsum, iron ore, natural gas, opals, salt, talc.

Main attractions

Vineyards in Barossa Valley and Clare Valley, Flinders Ranges, opal fields, Blue Lake/Mt Gambier, Kangaroo Island, Moonta and Burra Burra copper mine sites, The Barrages at Goolwa, Victor Harbor, Nullarbor Plain, whale-watching.

Flag

Based on the Blue Ensign with the state badge superimposed on the right-hand side. It consists of a piping shrike with wings outstretched on a yellow background.

Coat of arms

The present coat of arms was conferred by Queen Elizabeth II in 1984. It incorporates objects representing all aspects of industry in South Australia. At the base is a scroll with the words 'South Australia'.

Emblems

Animal: hairy-nosed wombat
Floral: Sturt's desert pea

Major festivals

January	Hahndorf German Shooting Festival
	Tanunda Oom-pah Festival
February	Adelaide Festival of the Arts
	(even-numbered years)
April	Barossa Valley Vintage Festival
May	Moonta Cornish Festival
November	Adelaide Christmas Pageant

DID YOU KNOW?
In 1862 John McDouall Stuart won 2000 pounds for finding a possible route between South Australia and the northern coastline. The Postmaster General of South Australia offered the reward in an attempt to establish an overland telegraph. This was completed in 1872.

Western Australia

Western Australia occupies the western third of the continent bordered by the Indian Ocean in the west and the Southern Ocean in the south.

Area

It is the largest state in Australia and is 2 252 500 square km in area.

Landform

The state extends from vast arable southern areas to semi-arid and arid landscapes in the interior and the mineral-rich Great Sandy and Gibson deserts to the north. The mountain ranges are Stirling, Kimberley and Hamersley.

Population

1 831 399 (concentrated on the south-west coast), representing only 9% of the total Australian population. The

large desert and semiarid areas are unsuitable for cultivation or close settlement.

Climate

Western Australia has three broad climate divisions. The northern part is dry tropical, receiving summer rainfall. The south-western corner has a Mediterranean climate with long hot summers and wet winters. The remainder is mostly arid land with desert climates. Average daily hours of sunshine, 7.9.

State capital

Perth is situated on the Swan River on the seaboard of the Indian Ocean. It is 5306 square km in area and has a population of 1 341 914.

Largest cities

Perth	1 341 914
Boulder-Kalgoorlie	31 391
Bunbury	28 069
Fremantle	25 540
Geraldton	20 353
Albany	15 775
Port Hedland	13 286

Industry

In Western Australia, health, education, cultural and other services, government and utilities account for 56% of the contribution to gross state product, the balance coming from mining 15%, wholesale and retail 14%, manufacturing 10% and primary industry 5%.

Chief products

Agriculture: cattle, fruit, hardwoods, rock lobsters, wheat, wool.
Manufacturing: building materials, food and drink, metal, machinery, other mineral products, petroleum products, wood products.
Mining: bauxite, gold, ilmenite, iron ore, nickel, oil, salt.

Main attractions

Margaret River, black swans, Kalgoorlie goldfields, Esperance, Mt Tom Price, Mt Newman, Ord River, Kimberley and Hamersley ranges, Broome, surfing, fishing, sailing, wildflowers, Monkey Mia (dolphins), Pinnacle Desert, Bungle Bungles.

Flag

The flag is based on the Blue Ensign with the badge of the

state superimposed on the right-hand side. It has a black swan within a yellow circle.

Coat of arms

The present coat of arms was granted by Queen Elizabeth II in 1969. It incorporates a shield depicting a black swan, the bird emblem of the state. It is supported by two kangaroos each holding a boomerang.

Emblems

Animal: numbat
Floral: red and green kangaroo paw

Major festivals

January	Perth Hyde Park Festival
February	Festival of Perth
March	Swan River Festival
August	Tom Price Nameless Festival
November	Fremantle Week

DID YOU KNOW?
In 1975, at Onslow in Western Australia, the wind velocity reached 246 km/h – the strongest wind ever recorded in Australia.

Tasmania

Location

The island state lies 240 km off the south-eastern corner of the Australian continent and is separated from the mainland by Bass Strait.

Area

Tasmania is the smallest state in Australia, with an area of 67 800 square km.

Landform

Mountainous with many lakes, waterfalls and steeply falling rivers.

Population

471 885, mostly on the north and east coasts.

Climate

Cool temperate with temperatures often falling below zero. There is high rainfall, very cold winters and cool summers. Average daily hours of sunshine, 5.8.

State capital

Hobart, the second-oldest city in Australia, is situated on the Derwent River on the Tasman Peninsula. It has an area of 936 square km and a population of 194 974.

Largest cities

Hobart	194 974
Launceston	98 352
Burnie and Devonport	78 605

Industry

In Tasmania, health, education, cultural and other services, government and utilities account for 62% of the contribution to gross state product, the balance coming from manufacturing 15%, wholesale and retail 15%, with the remainder spread over mining and primary industry.

Chief products

Agriculture: beef, canned fruit, dairy products, hops, lavender, mutton, potatoes, timber, wool.
Fishing: barracouta, crayfish, salmon, scallops.
Mining: coal, copper, gold, iron, lead, tin, zinc.

Main attractions

Snowfields, unspoiled mountain landscapes, historical places, national parks, fishing, Franklin River, seascapes, thermal pools, Gordon River.

Flag

Based on the Blue Ensign with the badge of the state superimposed on the right-hand side. It consists of a red lion in a white circle.

Coat of arms

The present coat of arms was granted by King George V in 1917. On the shield are pictures representing industry in Tasmania. This is supported by two Tasmanian tigers. The motto means 'Productiveness and faithfulness'.

Emblem

Floral: southern blue gum

Major festivals

January	Arrival of Sydney to Hobart Yacht Race
April	Statewide National Heritage Week
October	Devonport Rhododendron Festival
December	Hobart Salamanca Arts Festival

DID YOU KNOW?
Because Tasmanian bees are exclusive to the island and the pollen of the flowers is kept relatively pure, Tasmanian honey has a unique and distinctive taste.

Northern Territory

Location

The Northern Territory occupies a huge area of the continent's north and centre. It is bordered by the Timor Sea to the north, Queensland to the east, Western Australia to the west and South Australia to the south. Usually known as 'Outback Australia'.

Area

Comprises one-sixth of Australia's land mass and is 1 346 200 square km in area.

Landform

Mostly desert tablelands.

Population

189 991. Few people live in the huge dry areas and almost half the population are residents of Darwin. More than one quarter of the people are Aborigines.

Climate

The Northern Territory lies in the torrid zone. There are two broad climatic divisions: the northern part known as the 'Top End' receives heavy rainfall for three to five months of the year and the southern area, known as 'The Centre', has a low rainfall and no permanent rivers. Average daily hours of sunshine, 8.5.

Administrative centre

Darwin is situated in Beagle Gulf on the Timor Sea and is 1660 square km in area. It has a population of 86 576.

Chief towns

Darwin	86 576
Alice Springs	36 910
Katherine	9 856
Nhulunbuy	3 862
Tennant Creek	3 719

Industry

In the Northern Territory, health, education, cultural and other services, government and utilities account for 61% of the contribution to gross state product, the balance coming from mining 17%, wholesale and retail 13%, manufacturing 5% and primary industry 4%.

Chief products

Agriculture: beef cattle, citrus fruits, lucerne, peanuts, pineapples, timber, tomatoes.
Fishing: fish and prawns.
Mining: aluminium, bauxite, copper, gold, iron, manganese, tin, uranium.

Main attractions

Mt Olga National Park, Kings Canyon, Standley Chasm, *The Ghan* (train from Adelaide to Alice Springs), Katherine Gorge, Bathurst and Melville islands, Kakadu National Park, Uluru National Park (Ayers Rock), Devil's Marbles, Mataranka thermal pool, Litchfield National Park.

Flag

The flag of the Northern Territory is not based on the Blue Ensign. Instead, traditional Territory colours are used: black, white and red ochre. The stars on the black panel represent the Southern Cross. On the red ochre panel appears Sturt's desert rose.

Coat of arms

The present coat of arms was granted by Queen Elizabeth II in 1978. It incorporates a shield depicting an Arnhem Land rock painting of an Aboriginal woman. The shield is supported by two red kangaroos. The crest consists of a wedge-tailed eagle with wings splayed and its talons grasping an Aboriginal ritual stone or *tjurunga*.

Emblems

Animal: red kangaroo
Floral: Sturt's desert rose

Major festivals

May	Alice Springs Bangtail Muster
	Tennant Creek Lion's Gold Rush Festival
June	Katherine Carnival
July	Darwin Beer Can Regatta
August	Alice Springs Henley-on-Todd Regatta

DID YOU KNOW?
Alice Springs is almost the geographical centre of the continent in the great central desert. It is the focal point for the arid inland, more popularly known as the 'red centre'.

Famous Australians

Although there have been thousands of famous Australians, here is a very modest list of talented Australians, past and present, who have helped make this country what it is today.

Architects
Francis Greenway *(1777–1837)*
Colonel William Light *(1786–1839)*
Edmund Blacket *(1817–83)*
Walter Burley Griffin *(1876–1937)*
Sir Roy Grounds *(1905–81)*
Robin Boyd *(1919–71)*
Harry Seidler *(1923–)*

Aviators
Lawrence Hargrave *(1850–1915)*
Keith Smith *(1890–1955)*
Sir Hudson Fysh *(1895–1974)*

Ross Smith *(1892–1922)*
Bert Hinkler *(1892–1933)*
Sir Charles Kingsford Smith *(1897–1935)*
Amy Johnson *(1903–41)*
Sir Reginald Ansett *(1909–81)*

Businesspeople

John Macarthur *(1767–1834)*
Sir Warwick Fairfax *(1901–87)*
Herbert Cole 'Nugget' Coombs *(1906–97)*
Lang Hancock *(1909–92)*
Rupert Murdoch *(1931–)*
Robert Holmes à Court *(1937–90)*
Kerry Packer *(1937–)*

Cartoonists

Stan Cross *(1888–1977)*
Emile Mercier *(c. 1909–81)*
Frank Benier *(c. 1923–)*
Bruce Petty *(1929–)*
Ron Tandberg *(1943–)*
Michael Leunig *(1945–)*

Engineers & inventors

William James Farrer *(1845–1906)*
Herbert Lysaght *(1862–1940)*

John Bradfield *(1867–1943)*
Walter Hume *(1873–1943)*
Essington Lewis *(1881–1961)*
Mervyn Victor Richardson *(1894–1972)*
John Paul Wild *(1923–)*
Ralph Sarich *(1938–)*

Scientists & medicos

William Redfern *(c. 1774–1833)*
Reverend John Flynn *(1880–1951)*
Lord (Howard) Florey *(1898–1968)*
Sir Marcus Oliphant *(1901–)*
Sir John Eccles *(1903–)*
Sir Edward 'Weary' Dunlop *(1907–93)*
Professor Fred Hollows *(1929–93)*
Dr Victor Chang *(c. 1940–91)*
Dr Peter Douherty *(1941–)*
Dr Eric LePage *(1958–)*

Literature

Novelists and writers

Miles Franklin *(1879–1954)*
Henry Handel Richardson *(1870–1946)*
Xavier Herbert *(1901–84)*
Patrick White *(1912–90)*
Frank Hardy *(1917–94)*

Elizabeth Jolley *(1923–)*
Ruth Park *(1926–)*
David Ireland *(1927–)*
Christopher Koch *(1932–)*
David Malouf *(1934–)*
Thomas Keneally *(1935–)*
Helen Garner *(1942–)*
Peter Carey *(1943–)*
Kate Grenville *(1950–)*
Tim Winton *(1960–)*

Playwrights

Ray Lawler *(1922–)*
Richard Beynon *(1925–)*
Peter Kenna *(1930–)*
David Williamson *(1942–)*
Alexander Buzo *(1944–)*
Louis Nowra *(1950–)*

Poets

Andrew Barton 'Banjo' Paterson *(1864–1941)*
Dame Mary Gilmore *(1865–1962)*
Henry Lawson *(1867–1922)*
C. J. Dennis *(1876–1938)*
Kenneth Slessor *(1901–71)*
A. D. Hope *(1907–)*

Douglas Stewart *(1913–85)*
Judith Wright *(1915–)*
Oodgeroo of the tribe Noonuccal (formerly Kath Walker) *(1920–93)*

Theatre
J. C. Williamson *(1835–1913)*
Leo McKern *(1921–)*
Ruth Cracknell *(1926–)*
June Salter *(1932–)*
John Meillon *(1934–90)*
John Bell *(1940–)*
Jon Ewing *(1940–)*
Max Cullen *(1941–)*
Robyn Nevin *(1942–)*
John Waters *(1945–)*
Jacki Weaver *(1947–)*
Angie Milliken *(1968–)*

Radio
John Laws *(1935–)*
Bob Francis *(1938–)*
Rod Muir *(1941–)*
Margaret Throsby *(1942–)*
Bill Gates *(c. 1945–)*
Jeremy Cordeau *(1945–)*

Clive Robertson *(1945–)*
Howard Sattler *(1945–)*
Ian 'Macca' MacNamara *(1947–)*
Neil Mitchell *(1951–)*

Television
Hector Crawford *(1914–91)*
Brian Henderson *(1931–)*
Ernie Sigley *(1938–)*
Bert Newton *(1938–)*
Lorraine Bayly *(1939–)*
Mike Willesee *(1942–)*
Ray Martin *(1944–)*
Don Burke *(1948–)*
Daryl Somers *(1952–)*
Tony Martin *(1956–)*
Ernie Dingo *(1957–)*
Peter Phelps *(c. 1965–)*
Lisa McCune *(1971–)*

Film
Silent movies

Bert Bailey *(1872–1953)*
Arthur Tauchert *(1877–1933)*
Lottie Lyell *(1891–1925)*
George Wallace *(1894–1960)*

Early Talkies

Errol Flynn *(1909–59)*
Chips Rafferty *(1909–71)*
Peter Finch *(1915–77)*

Contemporary

Bill Hunter *(1939–)*
Paul Hogan *(1940–)*
Bryan Brown *(1948–)*
Sam Neill *(1948–)*
Geoffrey Rush *(1950–)*
Colin Friels *(1953–)*
Noni Hazlehurst *(1954–)*
Mel Gibson *(1956–)*
Greta Scacchi *(1957–)*
Hugo Weaving *(1960–)*
Russell Crowe *(1964–)*
Nicole Kidman *(1968–)*
Noah Taylor *(1969–)*
Cate Blanchett *(1972–)*
Rachel Griffiths *(1972–)*
Ben Mendelsohn *(1972–)*
Miranda Otto *(1973–)*
Toni Collette *(1973–)*
Matt Day *(1974–)*

Guy Pearce *(1974–)*
Frances O'Connor *(1976–)*

Film-makers

Patricia Lovell *(c. 1932–)*
Bruce Beresford *(1940–)*
Fred Schepisi *(1940–)*
Dean Semler *(1943–)*
Peter Weir *(1944–)*
George Miller *(1949–)*
Phillip Noyce *(1950–)*
Gillian Armstrong *(1950–)*
Rolf de Heer *(1951–)*
Laura Jones *(1951–)*
Byron Kennedy *(1952–83)*
Jane Campion *(1954–)*

Contemporary music
Rock

Johnny O'Keefe *(1935–78)*
Billy Thorpe *(c. 1940–)*
Jimmy Barnes *(1946–)*
Daryl Braithwaite *(1949–)*
John Farnham *(1949–)*
Ian Moss *(1950–)*
Archie Roach *(c. 1955–)*

Jenny Morris *(1957–)*
Nick Cave *(1958–)*
Paul Kelly *(1958–)*
Wendy Matthews *(1960–)*
Kate Ceberano *(1966–)*
Tina Arena *(1967–)*
Christine Anu *(c. 1968–)*
Kylie Minogue *(1968–)*
Natalie Imbruglia *(1975–)*

Country

Smoky Dawson *(1913–)*
Slim Dusty *(1927–)*
Reg Lindsay *(1929–)*
Jimmy Little *(1935–)*
Anne Kirkpatrick *(1952–)*
Graeme Connors *(1955–)*
Colin Buchanan *(1964–)*
Lee Kernaghan *(1964–)*
James Blundell *(1965–)*
Jane Saunders *(1965–)*
Troy Cassar-Daley *(1968–)*
Gina Jeffreys *(1968–)*

Rock bands

AC/DC
Air Supply
Angels
Australian Crawl
Baby Animals
Bee Gees
Black Sorrows
Chocolate Starfish
Cold Chisel
Crowded House
Daddy Cool
Divinyls
Easybeats
Hoodoo Gurus
Hunters and Collectors
Icehouse
INXS

Little River Band
Men at Work
Mental as Anything
Midnight Oil
Noiseworks
Regurgitator
Savage Garden
Screaming Jets
Sherbet
silverchair
Skyhooks
Southern Sons
Weddings, Parties,
  Anything
Whitlams
Yothu Yindi
You Am I

Other performers

Tommy Tycho *(1929–)*
Peter Allen *(1944–92)*
John Williamson *(1945–)*
Julie Anthony *(1951–)*
Tommy Emmanuel *(1955–)*
Debbie Byrne *(1958–)*
Jackie Love *(1961–)*
James Morrison *(1963–)*
Anthony Warlow *(1964–)*
Marina Pryor *(1964–)*
Nathan Cavaleri *(1982–)*

Classical music

Percy Grainger *(1882–1961)*
Peter Sculthorpe *(1929–)*
Richard Bonynge *(1930–)*
Nigel Butterley *(1935–)*
John Williams *(1941–)*
Roger Woodward *(1942–)*
Simone Young *(1962–)*
Karin Schaupp *(c. 1975–)*

Ballet & dance

Sir Robert Helpmann *(1909–86)*
Marilyn Jones *(1940–)*

Marilyn Rowe-Maver *(1946–)*
Graeme Murphy *(1950–)*
Garry Norman *(1951–)*
David Atkins *(1956–)*
Meryl Tankard *(c. 1957–)*
Lisa Pavane *(1962–)*
Greg Horsman *(1963–)*
Adam Marchant *(1963–)*
Steven Heathcote *(1965–)*
Miranda Coney *(1966–)*
Paul Mercurio *(c. 1967–)*
Vicki Attard *(c. 1967–)*
Justine Summers *(c. 1974–)*
Lisa Bolte *(c. 1975–)*

Opera
Dame Nellie Melba *(1861–1931)*
Dame Joan Sutherland *(1926–)*
Robert Allman *(1929–)*
Heather Begg *(1933–)*
Joan Carden *(c. 1939–)*
Donald Shanks *(1940–)*
Yvonne Kenny *(c. 1952–)*
Graham Pushee *(c. 1955–)*
Peter Coleman-Wright *(1959–)*
Cheryl Barker *(1960–)*

Art

Frederick McCubbin *(1855–1917)*
Tom Roberts *(1856–1931)*
Max Meldrum *(1875–1955)*
Norman Lindsay *(1879–1969)*
Margaret Preston *(1883–1963)*
Sali Herman *(1898–1993)*
Albert Namatjira *(1902–59)*
Sir Sidney Nolan *(1917–92)*
Arthur Boyd *(1920–)*
Judy Cassab *(1920–)*
Robert Klippel *(1920–)*
Sam Fullbrook *(1922–)*
Colin Lanceley *(1938–)*
Brett Whiteley *(1939–92)*
Trevor Nicholls *(1949–)*
Tim Storrier *(1949–)*

Major Australian films 1970-99

1971	*Wake in Fright*
1972	*The Adventures of Barry McKenzie*
1973	*Alvin Purple*
1974	*The Cars that Ate Paris*
1975	*Picnic at Hanging Rock*
	The Removalists
1976	*Caddie*
	Don's Party
1977	*The Getting of Wisdom*
1978	*My Brilliant Career*
	Newsfront
	The Chant of Jimmie Blacksmith
1979	*Mad Max*
	Breaker Morant
1981	*Puberty Blues*
1982	*Gallipoli*
	The Man from Snowy River
	The Year of Living Dangerously
1983	*Careful He Might Hear You*
1984	*My First Wife*
1985	*Bliss*
	Empty Beach
1986	*Backlash*
	Crocodile Dundee
	The Fringe Dwellers

1987	Boundaries of the Heart
	High Tide
	The Year My Voice Broke
1988	Crocodile Dundee II
	Dead Calm
1989	Jig Saw
	Sweetie
1990	The Crossing
	Flirting
1991	Death in Brunswick
1992	Fern Gully
	The Last Days of Chez Nous
	Strictly Ballroom
	Romper Stomper
1993	The Piano
1994	The Adventures of Priscilla, Queen of the Desert
	The Sum of Us
	Bad Boy Bubby
	Muriel's Wedding
1995	Lillian's Story
	The Seedling
	Babe
	Cosi
1996	Shine
	Love Serenade

Sporting Greats

Australia is a very enthusiastic sporting nation. We love our sport, whether watching or playing. Over the years we have had countless sporting legends who have shone in literally hundreds of different sports. Obviously, a book this size cannot hope to do justice to them all, so here are just some of them:

Tennis

Lawn tennis was first introduced in the 1870s and the first Australian championship was in 1905. The first Davis Cup challenge was in 1906. Tennis has become one of Australia's most popular sports. The following list names some of the greats:

1900–40s

Norman Brookes
Jack Crawford
Harry Hopman
Gerald Patterson
Adrian Quist

1950s–70s

John Bromwich
Roy Emerson
Neale Fraser
Lew Hoad
Rod Laver
Ken McGregor
John Newcombe
Tony Roche
Ken Rosewall
Frank Sedgman
Margaret Smith Court
Evonne Cawley (Goolagong)

1980s–

Pat Cash
Jelena Dokic
Scott Draper
Annabel Ellwood

Kerri-Ann Guse
Lleyton Hewitt
Andrew Ilie
Rachel McQuillan
Mark Philippoussis
Nicole Pratt
Patrick Rafter
Sandon Stolle
Jason Stoltenberg
Wendy Turnbull
Todd Woodbridge
Mark Woodforde

Cricket
The first organised match was held in Sydney in 1803. The Australian Club was formed in 1826 and the Melbourne Cricket Club in 1838. International cricket began in 1861.

1900–30s

G. W. Armstrong
Don Bradman
Bill Hunt
M. A. Noble
Bill O'Reilly
W. H. Ponsford
Hugh Trumble

1950s–70s

Ian Craig
Richie Benaud
Greg Chappell
Ian Chappell
Wally Grout
Neil Harvey
Lindsay Hassett
Bill Lawry
Ray Lindwall
Rod Marsh
Keith Miller
Bob Simpson

1980s–

David Boon
Allan Border
Ian Healy
Merv Hughes
Dennis Lillee
Geoff Marsh
Craig McDermott
Glenn McGrath
Mark Taylor
Shane Warne
Mark Waugh
Steve Waugh

Golf

Australians have more public courses per head of population than any other nation. The game was first played in 1870s and in 1890 the first established golf club was at Fallstaff Gardens in Melbourne.

1920s–1940s

Jim Ferrier
Joan Hammond
Joe Kirkwood
Norman von Nida
Ivo Whitton

1950s–1970s

Bruce Crampton
Bruce Devlin
Edwina Kennedy
Kel Nagle
Jack Newton
Peter Thomson

1980s–

Robert Allenby
Stuart Appleby
Ian Baker-Finch

Roger Davis
Steve Elkington
David Graham
Bradley Hughes
Graham Marsh
Greg Norman
Craig Parry
Peter Senior
Bob Shearer
Craig Spence
Jan Stephenson
Karrie Webb

Swimming

Because of our wonderful climate and beautiful beaches, Australians have always loved swimming. Swimming racing gained international fame when the 'Australian Crawl' (now called freestyle) was introduced in the 1890s.

1900–30s

Frank Beaurepaire
Barney Bede Kieran
Dick Cavill
Fred Cavill
Andrew ('Boy') Charlton
Claire Dennis

Fanny Durack
Annette Kellerman
Freddy Lane
Bill Longworth

1940s–60s

Kevin Berry
Gary Chapman
Lorraine Crapp
John Devitt
Dawn Fraser
John Henricks
John Konrads
Ilsa Konrads
Lynette McClements
Linda McGill
John Marshall
Ian O'Brien
Murray Rose
David Thiele
Mike Wenden
Robert Windle

1970s–80s

Duncan Armstrong

Clifford Bertram
Neil Brooks
Brad Cooper
Lisa Curry
Michelle Ford
Shane Gould
Gail Neal
Des Renford
Jon Sieben
Beverley Whitfield
Tracey Wickham

1990s–

Rebecca Brown
Grant Hackett
Michael Klim
Daniel Kowalski
Susie Maroney
David O'Brien
Susie O'Neill
Kieren Perkins
Samantha Riley
Shelley Taylor-Smith
Ian Thorpe
Joseph Walker
Tammy van Wisse

Australian Football League (AFL)

The game was devised in 1858 by cricketers as a form of exercise in their off-season. It has now become one of the most popular spectator sports in Australia. The AFL has inducted 12 legends into its Hall of Fame.

Roy Cazaly *(1910–27)*
Bob Pratt *(1930–46)*
Jack Dyer *(1931–49)*
Haydn Bunton *(1931–41)*
Dick Reynolds *(1933–51)*
John Coleman *(1949–54)*
Ted Whitten *(1951–70)*
Ron Barassi *(1955–77)*
Bob Skilton *(1956–71)*
Graham 'Polly' Farmer *(1956–60)*
John Nicholls *(1957–74)*
Leigh Matthews *(1969–85)*

National Rugby League (NRL)

The first Kangaroo team toured England in 1908–09 and won their first test in 1911–12. The Kangaroos have won the World Cup eight times out of the eleven tournaments played. Some greats of the game and the years they played are:

Herbert (Dally) Messenger *(1908–13)*
Duncan Thompson *(1911–25)*
Frank Burge *(1911–27)*
Harold Horder *(1912–26)*
Dave Brown *(1930–41)*
Vic Hey *(1933–49)*
Clive Churchill *(1951–63)*
John Raper *(1957–73)*
Ken Irvine *(1958–72)*
Reg Gasnier *(1959–67)*
Graeme Langlands *(1962–76)*
Keith 'Golden Boots' Barnes *(1963–70)*
Ron Coote *(1965–78)*
Arthur Beetson *(1966–81)*
Bob Fulton *(1965–79)*
Tom Radonikus *(1976–85)*
Wally Lewis *(1978–92)*
Mal Meninga *(1978–94)*
Peter Sterling *(1978–92)*
Allan Langer *(1986–99)*
Laurie Daley *(1987–)*
Ricky Stuart *(1988–)*
Brad Fittler *(1989–)*

Rugby Union

Rugby Union was first played in Australia in 1864. The first Wallabys team won gold at the 1908 London Olympics. The Wallabys won the World Cup Grand Slam tour in 1984 defeating England, Scotland, Wales and Ireland and in 1991 won the second World Cup championships. It remains an amateur game.

Some great names from the last three decades are:

Andrew Slack
Mark Ella
David Campese
Michael Lynagh
Nick Farr-Jones

Soccer

Although the game was played as early as 1880, it only gained prestige and popularity when the Australian team, the Socceroos, qualified, for the first time, in the World Cup finals in 1974. In later years, the Socceroos reached the finals of the Seoul, Barcelona and Atlanta Olympics. Some of Australia's soccer legends are:

Atti Abonyi
Mark Bosnich
Branko Buljevic
Alan Davidson

Craig Johnston
John Kosmina
Eddie Krncevic
Jim Mackay
Peter Ollerton
Jack Reilly
Jimmy Rooney
Paul Wade
Johnny Warren
Harry Williams
Peter Wilson
Charlie Yankos

Boxing

Bare-knuckle fights were staged in the 1790s but the rules
were standardised in 1912. Some of this century's greats
(and the dates they competed) are:

Bill Squires *(1907)*
Jerry Jerome *(1913)*
Les Darcy *(1916)*
Vic Patrick *(1945)*
Dave Sands *(1949)*
Vic Toweel *(1952)*
Jimmy Carruthers *(1952)*
Lionel Rose *(1968)*
Johnny Famechon *(1969)*

Rocky Mattioli *(1977)*
Jeff Fenech *(1985)*
Barry Michael *(1985)*
Lester Ellis *(1985)*
Joe Bugner *(1985)*
Jeff 'Hitman' Harding *(1989)*
Jeff Malcolm *(1994)*
Grahame 'Spike' Cheney *(1994)*
Kostya Tszyu *(1995)*

Melbourne Cup

This is the richest racing and spring social event in Australia. The race began in 1861 when the background of immense wealth from the gold fields created the climate for a race such as this. Archer was the first horse to win the Melbourne Cup.

1930	Phar Lap	1939	Rivette
1931	White Nose	1940	Old Rowley
1932	Peter Pan	1941	Skipton
1933	Hallmark	1942	Colonus
1934	Peter Pan	1943	Dark Felt
1935	Marabou	1944	Sirius
1936	Wotan	1945	Rainbird
1937	The Trump	1946	Russia
1938	Catalogue	1947	Hiraji

1948	Rimfire	1974	Think Big
1949	Foxzami	1975	Think Big
1950	Comic Court	1976	Van Der Hum
1951	Delta	1977	Gold and Black
1952	Dalray	1978	Arwon
1953	Wodalla	1979	Hyperno
1954	Rising Fast	1980	Beldale Ball
1955	Toparoa	1981	Just A Dash
1956	Evening Peal	1982	Gurner's Lane
1957	Straight Draw	1983	Kiwi
1958	Baystone	1984	Black Knight
1959	Macdougal	1985	What A Nuisance
1960	Hi Jinx	1986	At Talaq
1961	Lord Fury	1987	Kensei
1962	Even Stevens	1988	Empire Rose
1963	Gatum Gatum	1989	Tawrrific
1964	Polo Prince	1990	Kingston Rule
1965	Light Fingers	1991	Let's Elope
1966	Galilee	1992	Subzero
1967	Red Handed	1993	Vintage Crop
1968	Rain Lover	1994	Jeune
1969	Rain Lover	1995	Doriemus
1970	Baghdad Note	1996	Saintly
1971	Silver Knight	1997	Might And Power
1972	Piping Lane	1998	Jezabeel
1973	Gala Supreme		

Fauna

Mammals

Australia has about 230 species of mammals and almost half are marsupials, the pouched mammal. The balance consists of placental mammals (having a placenta which nourishes the embryo), and the monotremes, the lowest order of egg-laying mammals (having one opening for digestive, urinary and genital organs).

Marsupials

The **bandicoot** is a small animal resembling a native cat, but is insect-eating.

The **koala**, which is not a member of the bear family, lives in trees, drowsing during the day and becoming more active in the evening. It feeds on vast quantities of gum leaves which have a high oil content, enabling it to go for long periods without water. Its pouch opens downwards.

Kangaroos are represented in Australia by three subfamilies: Hypsiprymnodontinae, the Potoroinae and the Macropodinae. Its pouch opens upwards and it has a unique continuous flow of reproduction, with one joey outside the pouch which will still suckle, one inside suckling and one embryo 'on hold'. There are 45 species in Australia.

The **marsupial mole** is a small animal which lives in desert regions. It is eyeless and has no claws, unlike the true mole. It is rarely found because it lives underground.

The **numbat** is a unique striped marsupial now found only in the southwest corner of Western Australia. It is an endangered species because it is hunted by feral animals. It has sharp front claws and a sticky tongue with which it attacks ant and termite nests. Strangely, it has no pouch – the young cling with their mouths to the mother's underside until old enough to fend for themselves.

Possums are herbivorous marsupials which live in trees. They belong to four main families: ringtails and large gliders; brushtails and cuscus; feathertail and pygmy possums and honey possums.

The **Tasmanian devil** is the largest surviving carnivorous marsupial. It is nocturnal and very shy. It is the size of a fox terrier but has strength enough in its teeth to consume a whole sheep, including the skull. The litter can remain in the pouch for months.

Also known as thylacine, the **Tasmanian tiger** is the largest carnivorous marsupial in the world. It is presumed extinct although there are many unconfirmed sightings.

The **wombat** is a powerful, thickset, burrowing marsupial found only in Australia. Not a very sociable animal, it has a bony plate in its rump which can be used to kill any predator which might follow it into its burrow.

Placental mammals

In Australia, placental mammals (which produce fully developed young) comprise bats, dingoes, rodents and marine mammals.

The **bat** is the only true flying mammal. There are 58 species in Australia including the fruit bat and the rare ghost bat.

The **dingo** is a dog considered indigenous to Australia. It is presumed to have evolved from dogs brought from Asia 3000 to 8000 years ago by the ancestors of the Australian Aborigines. Dingoes are stealthy nocturnal hunters and often set up a continual chorus of howls much like the wolf.

Sea lions and **seals** are marine mammals found on Australia's southern coastline. **Dugongs** are herbivorous marine mammals which feed on sea grasses.

Monotremes

The **echidna** has sharp claws and a long sticky ribbon-like tongue with which it gathers up ants and termites at lightning speed. It has no teeth and relies on its stiff spines for protection. It lays a single egg which is carried and hatched in a temporary but commodious pouch formed from folds of skin.

The **platypus**, unique to Australia, is the only other egg-laying mammal in the world. It has been considered a living fossil and may be the missing link between reptiles and mammals. Its fur and tail are beaver-like, and it has webbed clawed feet and a duck-like bill which is fleshy and sensitive. The platypus lays eggs and suckles its young.

Reptiles and amphibians

Australia has about 140 species of snake, 360 species of lizard, 2 species of crocodile, 15 species of freshwater tortoise and 6 species of marine turtle.

Crocodiles

Both species are found in northern waters. The freshwater crocodile is not dangerous to people but the saltwater species, which can grow to 7 metres long, is very dangerous

Frogs

There are approximately 130 species of frog in Australia but no salamanders. Australia's native frogs include a diverse array of tree frogs, marsh frogs and burrowing frogs.

Lizards

Australian lizards range in size from 55 mm to 2.4 metres long. The great perentie or goanna is the second-largest lizard in the world. The most popular lizard is the frill-necked lizard which has a vivid frill of skin. Under attack it unfolds the frill, sways to and fro, opens its mouth wide and hisses. The blue-tongued lizard belongs to the skink family, the most prevalent lizard species in Australia.

Snakes

Only about 140 species of snake are found in Australia and about 100 of these are venomous. The nonvenomous snakes include pythons, blind snakes, file snakes and some colubrid snakes. Among the venomous snakes are the death adder, the tiger snake and the taipan.

Insects

Australia has over 50 000 species of insects. There are about 350 species of butterflies, 7600 species of moths,

18 000 species of beetles and 900 species of ants. There are over 200 species of cicadas.

Arachnids
The funnel-web spider is the most poisonous spider in Australia and the male is five times more toxic than the female. The male red back spider is one-third the size of the female and is reputed to be nonvenomous. The female is highly venomous.

Marine organisms
The Great Barrier Reef is the earth's largest structure created by living creatures. It is a complex ecological maze of fortress-like structures composed of dead coral over which the living coral forms a mantle. The living coral is made up of millions of polyps. These tiny marine animals grow and reproduce on the remains of their ancestors.

Blue-ringed octopus
These small octopuses are found over vast areas. They often take the colour of their background but when irritated light up electric-blue rings around their body. Normally they are not aggressive but can sting when disturbed and their sting can be fatal.

Crown-of-thorns starfish

This starfish is approximately 30 cm in diameter. It is not deadly but because its spines are quite toxic it is hard to handle.

Sea wasp

This creature is often referred to as the box jellyfish because of its cubic shape. It has a simple branched tentacle flowing from each corner of the cube which is extremely dangerous. It is considered to be the most poisonous creature in our seas – a sting causing death within minutes.

Birds

There are over 700 different kinds of birds in Australia including the bower-builders, the lyrebirds, magpies, butcher birds and song larks.

Bell bird

They have a loud bell-like note and are found in open forest and sheltered dells on the eastern coast.

Black swan

The black swan is unique to Australia and the only species of swan on the continent.

Bower bird

The satin bower bird is found only in Australia and New Guinea.

Brolga

This is the only Australian crane. It is a swamp dweller found mostly on the inland plains.

Emu

The emu is the unofficial emblem of Australia. It is flight-less and stands about 1.5 metres high. It is closely related to the cassowary and next in size to the ostrich.

Honeyeater

The helmeted honeyeater is one of the rarest birds in the world. It is only found in southern Victoria, east of Port Phillip Bay.

Kookaburra

Unique to Australia, these birds are the largest of the king-fishers. There are two types, the laughing jackass of the eastern states and the blue-winged kookaburra of the north and north-west.

Lyrebird

Male lyrebirds have a fancy gauze-like tail, giving this unique bird its name. Lyrebirds are ground feeders and build incubation mounds for nests. They have a wide vocal range and are splendid mimics.

Parrots

There are more than 50 species of Australian parrots. Among them are galahs, sulphur-crested cockatoos, rosellas, lorikeets and budgerigars.

Penguin

The only penguin species residing in Australian waters is the fairy or little penguin. Phillip Island in Victoria is the home of the best known colony.

Swift & Swallow

The migratory spine-tailed swift is known as the storm bird, because it is often seen before and after a storm, feeding on the insects trapped in the air currents. The welcome swallow spends long hours soaring. These birds can feed their young without alighting on the nest.

Wedge-tailed eagle

With an average wingspan of 2.5 metres, this is Australia's largest raptor. It is found throughout Australia but is more common in the arid centre.

Flora

Although Australia is predominantly arid, with vast desert areas, there are many other vegetation regions such as rainforests, savanna grasslands, scrub, mallee, heath and alpine areas.

Australian plants in general are characterised by their drought-resistant qualities – tough spiny leaves and thick bark to resist evaporation. They are also very fire-resistant and many of these plants need a fierce fire to germinate seeds and rejuvenate.

The Australian land flora comprises over 12 000 species of flowering plants and is dominated by the eucalyptus (over 550 recognised species), paperbark, tea tree, banksia, wattle, casuarina and blackboy (grass tree).

Forests

On the northern and eastern coastlines of the Australian continent are vast areas of forest which experience rainfall ranging from 1000 to 2500 mm per year. The broad-leaved rainforests of the north are dominated by buttressing fig trees, interlacing lianas, cabbage fan palms and fungi, producing a dark and brooding atmosphere.

The open forests around the top end of the Northern Territory and on the east coast are less formidable and dense. Here, eucalypts such as mountain ash, spotted gum and hoop pine dominate the landscape.

Grasses and woodlands

These areas of Australia are to be found mainly 200 to 300 km inland from the north and east coasts. There is a greater distance between the trees here than in the forests, and tree crowns are quite large. Here the eucalypt abounds.

Scrub and mallee

This is a diverse community of shrubby plants where the most dominant, the mallee eucalyptus, is not more than 8 metres high. It is restricted to the south-eastern and south-western regions of the country where many Australian wildflowers grow.

Deserts

The true desert prevails over vast regions of the inland. Here the land receives unpredictable and extremely low rainfall, temperatures are extreme, and the evaporation exceeds precipitation. These adverse conditions not only create a variety of dry salt lakes and dry riverbeds but produce a complex mosaic of plant communities. Plants adapt by growing spindly leaves and tough bark to prevent evaporation.

Acknowledgements

When preparing a book such as this, there is always a considerable number of people who help with advice and information, and I sincerely thank them all. In particular, I would like to thank the staff of the following organisations: Australian Ballet; Opera Australia; Australian National Library; Mitchell Library; Department of Aboriginal Affairs; Department of the Prime Minister and Cabinet; Parliament House Education Resource, ACT; and the Premier's Department in each state.

I am also indebted to the following people for detailed information in specialised areas: Russell Best (flora and fauna); Kate Reynolds (ballet); Claire Vince (opera); Pat Yardley (art); Mark Hughes (rock music); Ross Dundas (cricket); Des Renford (swimming); and Pat Conlan (films).

List of Sources

Most of the information for this book has been adapted from the author's *The Little Aussie Fact Book* (also published by Penguin Books Australia), a larger, more detailed look at Australian facts and figures.

The author acknowledges indebtedness to the following books, which were consulted for reference:

Adams, K. M. *Australia: Colonies to the Commonwealth 1850–1900*. Angus & Robertson, 1990.

Aitken, Don & Jinks, Brian. *Australian Political Institutions*. Pitman, 1985.

Australian Museum. *The Complete Book of Australian Mammals*. Angus & Robertson, 1990.

Blanch, John. *Ampol Australian Sporting Records*. John Pollard, 1987.

Cayley, N. W. *What Bird is That?* Angus & Robertson, 1995.

Cheers, Gordon, et al. *Australia Through Time.* Random House, 1998.

—— *Australian Sport Through Time.* Random House, 1997.

Cronin, L. *Key Guide to Australian Trees.* Reed, 1997.

—— *Key Guide to Australian Wildflowers.* Reed, 1995.

Draper, W. J. (ed.). *Who's Who in Australia.* Herald & Weekly Times, 1984.

Fraser, Bryce (ed.). *The Macquarie Book of Events.* Macquarie Library, 1990.

Gleeson, James. *Australian Painters.* Lansdowne, 1989.

Shaw, John. *Australian Encyclopaedia.* Collins, 1984.

Simpson, Ken, Day, Nicolas, and Trusler, Peter. *A Field Guide to the Birds of Australia.* Viking, 1999.

Stratton, David. *The Avocado Plantation.* Pan Macmillan, 1990.

United Nations. *Demographic Yearbook.* 1998.

Facts and figures on demographics and the economy are from the Australian Bureau of Statistics and the Australian Stock Exchange.